Endorsements

Dr. Carol Lynch's long experience embodying, teaching, practicing, and living the principles of Science of Mind has naturally brought forth a book, *Jump into Spirit: How Our Sacred Connections Enhance Our Lives*. In it, she inspires us to deepen our connection to Source and to live a Spirit-led life, using clear and useful spiritual practices which are based on her own success. Her spiritual mind treatments are empowering resources for daily practice, a beautiful means to clear out unwanted patterns of belief while developing new mental and spiritual concepts of Reality that lift consciousness to a higher vibration of Truth. Open this book and jump right in!

Rev. Dr. Maxine Kaye, Author, *Alive and Ageless: How to Feel Alive and Live Fully Every Day of Your Life*

Dr. Ernest Holmes wrote, "One of the great difficulties in the new order of thought is that we are likely to indulge in too much theory and too little practice." This is the reason we need *Jump into Spirit: How Our Sacred Connections Enhance Our Lives*. In my years of ministry, people have often asked, "Okay, you've given me the why. What about the how? What should I do with all this theory?" The answer is here. Along with the why comes the how––practical methods for using the theory to bring about the positive change we desire in our lives. This book doesn't belong on your bookshelf; it belongs in front of you, open and read.

Rev. Michael Sternlieb, Spiritual Leader, Center for Spiritual Living Long Island

Dr. Carol Lynch, in her heartfelt approach to life, shares her wisdom based on knowing her Self. In this awareness shared with the language of love, she invites her readers to step over the threshold of Truth, the Truth about our God-expressed individuality, which is inherent in all of us but not always recognized. Her book delightfully elevates her readers' enthusiasm for the sacred intimacy we all yearn for when discovering the Truth of our being. *Jump into Spirit: How Our Sacred Connections Enhance Our Lives.* Is a genuine and loving reminder that wherever we go, God is ever-present; therefore, wherever we are is home.

Elena Maria Urban

This wonderful book is a wisdom adventure. Dr. Carol Lynch's story is a focus on God-given ideas and you will, by her example, discover how to mentally choose and spiritually decide what your life shall be. Every page shows you that your fulfillment in any and all areas of life is up to you. As you move through the power of the lessons entailed in *Jump into Spirit: How Our Sacred Connections Enhance Our Lives*, you will gratefully be convinced that the Higher Understanding within the author's words are good enough to be true. This book reflects Carol's New Thought genius and metaphysical substance. It is the perfect embodiment of intelligent thought.

Dr. Jay Scott Neale, Founder and Pastor, Tri-City Religious Science Center

Dr. Carol Lynch has created a book that will guide you on this journey we call Life. *Jump into Spirit: How Our Sacred Connections Enhance Our Lives* is a book that provides you the "tools" to change the quality of your life. Open it, read it, and––most importantly––practice the gifts you are being given.

Rev. Loretta Brooks, Director of Centers for Spiritual Living, New York City

Jump into Spirit: How Our Sacred Connections Enhance Our Lives is an exquisite read. If you are looking for the inspiration to take your spiritual quest to the next level, look no further. Dr. Carol Lynch is a seasoned guide because she has already been there. She not only points the way—she takes you by the hand and gently guides you to your next great "yet to be." You'll discover, in a new way, the authentic sacred the Self you have always been patiently awaiting your arrival. That is when the real fun begins as you "Jump into Spirit" with full abandon.

Dr. Dennis Merritt Jones, Author, *The Art of Abundance––Ten Rules for a Prosperous Life* and *The Art of Uncertainty––How to Live in the Mystery of Life and Love It.*

Dr. Carol Lynch has captured within the pages of her new book, *Jumping Into Spirit,* the wonderfully pure teachings taught by or our metaphysical grandparents who were so dedicated to Principle. Dr. Carol encourages us to remember *why* we lean on Metaphysical Principles and then guides us through the *how.* Her devotion to the purest aspects of our teaching is a beautiful and brilliant reminder of this gift we all enjoy so much – *The Science of Mind!*

I feel reminded to go back to Spirit and the Law, to lean on the ancient teachings to shift my life through the practice of shifting consciousness.

This book is perfect for the new and experienced student of the Metaphysics. For the new student, it is a great, *how to;* for the experienced student, it is a *wonderful reminder.* Thank you, Dr. Carol Lynch, for bringing this powerhouse book to the world.

Rev. Michelle Wadleigh, Spiritual Leader, Center for Spiritual Living North Jersey

Jump into Spirit

How Our
Sacred Connections
Enhance Our Lives

Carol Lynch

BALBOA.PRESS
A DIVISION OF HAY HOUSE

Balboa Press books may be ordered through booksellers or by contacting:

Balboa Press
A Division of Hay House
1663 Liberty Drive
Bloomington, IN 47403
www.balboapress.com
844-682-1282

Print information available on the last page.

Scripture taken from the King James Version of the Bible.

ISBN: 978-1-9822-3651-9 (sc)
ISBN: 978-1-9822-3652-6 (e)

Balboa Press rev. date: 01/27/2021

Contents

Acknowledgements.. ix
Foreword... xi
Introduction... xiii

1   Sacred Connections 1
2   Finding the Way 9
3   Creating the Bearable... 21
4   The Power of Love 31
5   Developing a Prosperity Consciousness................................... 39
6   Jumping into Spirit 51
7   The Path to Healing and Forgiveness.......................................61
8   The Law of Attraction 71
9   Everything Begins with an Idea 79
10 What Is Your Concept of God?... 87
11 The Journey Continues.. 95

Appendix: A Tribute to Louise Hay...103
A Tribute to The Rev. Dr. Wade Adkisson 107
Suggested Reading 109

Acknowledgements

To my beloved son, Eric, who taught me so much and brought joy to my life, which continues with his son––my grandson, Eli.

To Carl for his lifetime support.

To my cousin, Liz, who helped me through the Unbearable.

To the Rev Wade Adkisson who inspired me to the ministry.

To Rev. Dr. Cynthia Cavalcanti, my editor and friend who has guided me through the process with her gracious style. She is a joy to work with.

My gratitude to Rev. Elizabeth Arrott for her enthusiasm in writing the foreword.

Thanks and blessings to my endorsers for their time and support: Elena Urban, Rev. Loretta Brooks, Rev. Michelle Wadleigh, Rev. Dr. Maxine Kaye, Dr. Dennis Merritt Jones, Dr. Jay Scott Neale, and Rev. Michael Sternlieb.

To all of my students, interns, clients, colleagues and all those who have touched my life.

Foreword

Wow! *Jump into Spirit* . . . what an absolutely amazing concept!

But, how do we do it? When do we do it? And what happens when we do it? Well, we are about to find out.

That being said, the answer to each of the above questions is yours and yours alone. To make the whole thing even better, "jumping" is your own individual experience, unlike that of anyone else. That's because it's strictly between you and—you guessed it—Spirit.

First, let's lay a little groundwork. Most of us recognized early on that life is a journey and not a destination. This is a book about life and living. It is a book about *you*. And, yet, your hopes, desires, dreams, and, yes, your fears, are shared by all people in ways *that are unique to them*.

Living fully and joyously is probably one of the most sought-after goals of all time. We all want similar intangible qualities and expressions in our lives (such as happiness, self-esteem, success, and good health) but we achieve them individually—and differently.

All of us wonder what the "real deal" is in experiencing a rewarding and satisfying life. In our efforts to pick the road most likely to take us to the wonderful life we dream about, we debate our choices, our friends, our jobs, and certainly our educations. We ask other people. We look to see what works for them. We read the books they recommend. We learn, and we try. . . well, we try one thing after the other.

Dr. Carol Lynch is a rare combination. She is a highly trained minister and a highly trained doctoral-level psychologist as well. She lives successfully. And, she lives passionately, filled with purpose and expression.

In this book, she shares the primary things that have allowed her to move into a life of full expression. She also shares the fairly recent time in her life that was most challenging–– a virtually unbearable loss.

The answer to both--the full expression and the virtually unbearable--is the same. *Jump into Spirit.* The answer is a continuous one. *Jump into Spirit.* The sacred connections are always there because the One Spiritual Connection is there for each one of us, always ready to support us at exactly the right time—and responding to our call.

In strong and powerful words, Dr. Carol gives deeply meaningful examples of affirmative prayers we can use for ourselves in handling these individual moments in time. This is a book to be carefully read and studied. The message is simple. The understanding of the message changes as we grow in our own lives.

Elizabeth Rann Arrott
Co-Author, *Shortcut to a Miracle: How to Change Your Consciousness and Transform Your Life*

Introduction

My friend, Carol Lynch, is an amazing woman. She is brilliant, educated, and accomplished, and she is kind, compassionate, and supportive. She is beautiful in every sense of the word.

Carol's belief system turns on the notion that there is a Power for Good in the Universe. For some people, simply knowing this is enough. Not for Carol. She demands of herself a willingness to put her knowing into practice. While many of us are content just to think about spiritual concepts, she is assimilating them and taking action.

The average distance between the human head and the human heart is 18 inches. Figuratively speaking, that distance might as well be 100 miles for most people when it comes to embodying sacred knowledge. Again, not for Carol. She has a rare ability to live and love in accordance with the divine principles she espouses.

What if we could do that, too? And what if it were easy?

Well, we can. And it is easy––when we have someone to show us how.

Being the gifted teacher she is, Carol shows us how in *Jump into Spirit*. In this wonderful book, she guides us along the path of Truth toward an expanded expression of Life.

Carol has poured her authenticity into these pages in a way that is at once vulnerable and powerful. She is willing to show her pain, all the while allowing her strength to shine through because it is crucial that we witness both.

In every chapter, Carol draws from personal experiences that are relatable. She then elucidates the spiritual principle with which we must align to bring forth our desired good. After that, she bestows a treasure: affirmative prayers––called Spiritual Mind Treatments––that we can immediately use to center ourselves in the Truth of our being.

If you are ready to effect positive change in your life, allow Carol to take you by the hand and lead you, chapter by chapter, toward more love, prosperity, health, and joy. Go ahead––jump into Spirit!

Cynthia Cavalcanti
Laguna Beach, California

"There is no place that God is not . . . In a world in which this divine intelligence creates everything, there can be no accidents."

– Dr. Wayne Dyer

Chapter 1
Sacred Connections

What are Sacred Connections, and why are they important in our lives? All things are sacred. We are one with the One, and our oneness defines what we are—spiritual beings in human form. This book is an attempt to show how the Divine Presence unfolds in our lives and brings the right people—and the right experiences—to us at the right time.

In this book, I have included Spiritual Mind Treatments that have been used in my practice; this is our form of prayer in the Science of Mind teaching. Many of these were printed in *Creative Thought Magazine*, a spiritual periodical that was in publication for many decades. They are for your use and to help you develop your own positive prayer technique.

In my work as a psychologist and minister, I heard a lot of what goes on in other people's heads. For example, everyone wants love, but negativity—our own or another's often subverts us. We get stuck. Spirituality is freeing because it requires opening our hearts and doing our best to see every moment of life through the lens of Truth. We are all points of light, bonded together in our oneness. Let us wake up to this truth—the truth of our being—and live the greater life and be a center of peace.

Jumping into Spirit is an awakening to the idea that "It's all God," and that everything is sacred. However, as individualizations of the One, we have personalities and differences. Recognizing the sacred connections in our lives allows us to see the action of Spirit and how the connections impact our thinking, our feeling, and our lives. It shows how the law of attraction is working for us.

We teach that there is only One Mind; however, this mind is both Conscious/ Objective and Subconscious/Subjective. Ernest Holmes tells us that Conscious Mind is "the Self-knowing Mind in God or in man . . . the One Mind common to all men."

Subconscious Mind is soul; it is the way your mind acts. It receives, reacts, and creates. It always says yes to whatever you put into it. It can only reason deductively. It is connected to the collective consciousness of all humankind. Since Conscious Mind can change Subconscious Mind, our treatments work on this premise. If we change our thoughts, we can change our lives. This is why I have included in this book examples of Spiritual Mind Treatment for your use.

Sometimes life throws us curve balls—we lose a job, experience an unexpected death, or go through the break up of a relationship. This is what makes our teaching and the use of Spiritual Mind Treatment so valuable, as it gives us the tools to deal with whatever change comes our way.

Change always brings an opportunity to jump into a deeper level of being by jumping into Spirit. We find fresh new activity and let go of any judgments, grudges, or superficial thoughts. We change our erroneous beliefs and replace them with powerful, truth-centered beliefs. We move into congruity with our original nature, the harmony of life.

How do we do this?

We start by recognizing that we live in a universe of energy. Energy is everywhere. Our bodies are energy in action. We live in a universe of power, and we learn how to use it.

We have to believe in ourselves and our ability to achieve and accomplish.

We develop a spiritual confidence that allows us to recognize there is a power principle. We are in it and of it, and we express it in our affairs. We are all identical in our relationship to this power principle, yet the way we use it and express it is uniquely personal.

We recognize this power, its essence. It is our being, and we express it. If we are consciously aware of it, we conduct it.

We have to purge ourselves of the negative thoughts from the collective consciousness that bombard us. We let go of victim consciousness and embrace the change. When negative thoughts appear, say Stop It! Use a Spiritual Mind Treatment. We can also use meditation to quiet the mind and center ourselves. Take a positive thought and focus on it. Put your mind at ease. I find some quiet meditation to be helpful before doing treatments.

Spiritual Mind Treatment is a conscious movement of thought within the mind of the one praying. We do not send thoughts; all of the action is within the mind of the one praying. Each treatment has a goal or definite purpose. We are not pleading with a God outside ourselves. We create a spiritual awareness that leads us to a spiritual acceptance. We deny all blockages and affirm that our desired good is moving through the great Creative Intelligence to demonstrate in our lives.

To jump into spirit, we must experiment with these ideas and awaken to the presence within. Demonstration depends on our level of acceptance of these ideas. Look at your life and discover the sacred connections that have shaped your direction. Give thanks for the good received and bless your awakening.

If you are ready, jump in!

Spiritual Mind Treatments
for Sacred Connection

"Positive self-awareness is the cause of a perfect harmonious and beautiful life."

– Jay Scott Neale, *The Power of Positive Purpose*

I Live in Harmony

All is God, All is Good, All is Peace, and All is Love. It is that love unfolding that gently caresses me as I recognize this positive self-awareness. A joy arises within me that heals all darkness and confusion and releases them to the light. The light radiates as me and casts its warmth to all in my presence. It is the action of Spirit manifesting as a state of inner peace.

Life moves forward in beauty and reflects my new way of being. A new spiritual confidence opens me to new avenues of expression. It is the Oneness of being and the knowing that it is all God, it is all Good and it is God in action as me. It is my new way of thinking that casts out the doubt. It is my way of living in harmony and joy.

As I reflect on my deeper realization, I express gratitude to the Divine Presence within me for revealing this happy and harmonious action in my life today. I joyously accept this gift of a beautiful life. And so it is.

"To believe your own thought, to believe what is true for you in your private heart is true for all men...that is genius."

— Ralph Waldo Emerson, "Self-Reliance"

I Take Charge

The Power and Presence of God is all there is. Life is the unfolding action of God, moving in, through, and around me. As I recognize this Truth, I take charge and affirm my faith and belief in the Divine Presence within.

Love lights the way. Rejoicing in the renewed feeling of taking charge of my thinking, I relax and enjoy the Divine flow bringing a new beginning for my creative action. Any thought of limitation is released, for I know I am enough.

My belief in myself results in demonstrations of good and greater good. Expanded wealth, health, and love bless me as faith allows joyous action to open my heart and freely receive God's gifts moment by moment.

Love blossoms forth as the Divine Presence within me. I celebrate this Truth, and with great thanks, I declare it so. And so it is.

"Love operates in all of my relationships, from the most casual to the most intimate."

– Louise L. Hay

Chapter 2

Finding the Way

I remember the day well. It was winter, and I was six years old, recovering from scarlet fever. My aunt Ann came to visit and brought me the gift of a mustard seed pendant. Her message to me was, "Have faith."

I was raised Catholic, and the Church provided support to families and the community, which included my grandparents, aunts, and uncles. Everyone knew everyone else's business.

The church dominated our neighborhood with its high steeple and its message of fear. There was a God who watched over us. "He" knew everything we did and could punish us with the quickness of lightening.

In my mind, I had some lovely images of heaven—puffy white clouds and the angels with their harps. At the same time, I imagined the devil behind every tree, ready to pounce and deliver me to hell.

I attended Catholic high school, and it was then that I began to question my faith. During my college years, I explored Buddhism. It wasn't until many years later, when I was living in a carriage house in Llewellyn Park, in West Orange, New Jersey that I heard Dr. Raymond Charles Barker speaking on the radio. He was giving a talk entitled, "Yesterday Ended Last Night." I was intrigued.

Dr. Barker's concept of God was as one of Love and Law. He emphasized minimizing fear and maximizing faith. I said to myself, this is believable! I started to listen to his lessons on a regular basis and soon subscribed to *Creative Thought* and *Science of Mind* magazines.

I eventually made my way to Alice Tully Hall in New York City, where the First Church of Religious Science held its services. It was close to the time of Dr. Barker's retirement, and I attended his going-away dinner at the Chrysler Building. I joined First Church in 1979 when Dr. Stuart Grayson became pastor. I left the church in 1989 when I was remarried.

During the eighties, I was a school psychologist, working in the Bloomfield Public Schools. I was also a student in New York University's doctoral program in psychology.

My school district sent me to a workshop on the Meyers-Briggs Type indicator, which measures psychological preferences in how people see the world and make decisions. It is based on Carl Jung's book on psychological types. The assumption of the scale is that we all have specific preferences in the way we construe our experiences, and these preferences underlie our interests, needs, values, and motivations.

I came out on the scale as someone suited to ministry. I remember thinking it must be a mistake, yet many years later, I found myself studying for ministry.

I chose the path of Science of Mind because that teaching made sense to me. It explained the world and God in a logical way. It presented something I could believe, and after putting it into practice in my life—and reaping the benefits—I felt sure it was true.

Whether or not it is true, it's a beautiful way to live life. We all have challenges to face in our lives, and this teaching offers a way to deal with whatever those may be by using an affirmative form of prayer, Spiritual Mind Treatment. Treatment is a way to keep our minds focused on solutions rather than believing in luck, chance, or karma.

Each challenge presented teaches us a lesson. There are no sins; only mistakes. We study the law of attraction and ways that our thinking creates our lives, accepting the responsibility and seeking what works. There are no coincidences. Early on, I found the teaching very helpful during my divorce and through challenges I experienced with my son.

During psychotherapy with a counselor meeting with my son and me, we developed some strategies to ease the transition. She explored with me some of my childhood experiences and what led to my career and the changes I had made. We discussed my childhood dream of becoming an Egyptologist or detective, and how I loved reading books about Egypt and mystery novels.

As my high school graduation drew near, my parents said they would support my becoming a nurse, secretary, or teacher, but they really wanted me to get married. This was in the 1960s. I tried nursing, and decided it was not for me. I went to college and became a teacher.

I got married and had one son, Eric. When my marriage ended in divorce, I found my way back to Religious Science. I attended a Sunday meeting where I met Rev. Wade Adkisson, Dr. Stuart Grayson's successor.

I soon began my studies at the Institute of Religious Science in New York City. It was a long road, and I was willing to follow it. Some unexpected events brought some defining moments, including the terrorist attack on September 11th, which changed all of our lives in America.

I was invited to join the ministers at First Church in the counseling sessions and meetings we held for the victims and families at our location on 48th Street in New York City. That's was when I decided I would pursue the ministry, realizing the Science of Mind teaching is a spiritual psychology, and I was already licensed as a psychologist.

It is said when the student is ready, the teacher appears. For me, Rev. Adkisson was that teacher. He provided the inspiration and the contacts. Through his classes and instruction, the ideas unfolded for me and brought some of the most brilliant, loving, and supportive people into my life, including Louise Hay and Dr. Wayne Dyer.

At our Annual Asilomar Conference in Pacific Grove, California, Rev. Wade introduced me to all his colleagues, a great initiation into a wonderful group of ministers, including Dr. Jay Scott Neale, who had studied with Fenwicke Holmes, the brother of Ernest Holmes, the founder of Religious Science. Dr. Jay became a friend and mentor. It was indeed a new beginning, quite different from my life in the world of public schools.

I was taught from birth that life can be risky business, as my Catholic parents established for me a litany of fear-based limitations that were well meaning yet played a part in inhibiting my expression of authentic self. Through the practice of Science of Mind, I had many demonstrations and successes far beyond my initial expectations.

Having faith and belief––beginning with my childhood mustard seed gift, and, later, with the discovery of the Science of Mind teaching––moved me to pursue my goals and professional advancement. It also assisted me in letting go of many of the fears and empowered me to take risks. The right people at the right time showed up, and I attracted what I desired: two trips to Egypt, a doctoral degree in psychology, becoming a licensed practitioner and an ordained minister, and a trip to Tucson, Arizona, where I studied with Dr. Wayne Dyer and Louise Hay. Ernest Holmes' concept of spiritual psychology became very clear for me.

Each of us individualizes the presence of God, and we activate the law of cause and effect. With this recognition, and with defining our moments, we change the risky, chancy way of life. We realize that what we are thinking through our consciousness produces as an effect. We are always beneficiaries of the love of God and the law of God. Many people never come to this awareness. Spirit is always giving to itself by means of each one of us.

We create our own experience through our own individualized thinking. Our misuse of our thinking creates our difficulty and our hard choices. A positive thought creates a positive effect. It is a result of our Divine right to choose.

Do you believe life is filled with risky business, or defining moments? What we generally expect out of life is what we experience. For example, we can choose to be kind or to be right; we can choose to be peaceful or to be stressed. All such choices carry an inevitable effect. There are no accidents, only choices that are effects operating out of ignorance. We must be wise in our choices and operate from intelligence rather than emotion alone. Otherwise, we will suffer the consequences.

Thanks to Science of Mind, I know I can change my consciousness. Conscious mind can change subconscious mind! How? By using affirmative prayer, i.e., Spiritual Mind Treatment. Through treatment, we can create for ourselves that which we desire. We live under the law of God, and we are the product of our own thinking. Life can be a blessing or a curse depending on what we choose. By paying attention to our defining moments, we can move out of risky business. We are punished by our mistakes. If we choose to think or do wrong, we produce the wrong effect; by choosing right, we produce the right effect.

Through our study of Science of Mind, we take charge of our thinking and our actions. We define what we are doing in every moment. As we take control, our lives change. We are always unfolding. We are those wonderful individualizations of Spirit who are always Divinely connected.

By engaging in thinking that brings us our highest and greatest good, we realize everything we need is already present right here within us. Nothing happens by chance. Life only becomes risky business when we are not in the business of God. We must rise above the collective consciousness and be the independent thinker who defines life. We lift ourselves out of the negative thinking, out of "they say."

How do we accomplish this? By liking what we know about ourselves. Each of us is a mighty moving power of God in expression. Consciousness is the only reality, we can change any negative pattern through our treatment work and our belief. The deciding factor is the individual, and we are at choice.

Freedom is a core value, and Ernest Holmes maintains, "real freedom means that man is created in the image of perfection and let alone and allowed to make the discovery for himself." The one freedom that perhaps we take for granted more than any other is the underlying freedom to think a thought and then change our mind if that thought does not serve us well.

Awakening to the awareness that we can think and are always thinking some type of thought takes us out of bondage and into freedom. Understanding that our very next thought will either hold us hostage to our own habitual thinking or set us free is what the Science of Mind teaching is all about.

Spiritual Mind Treatments
for Finding the Way

"Everything comes from Intelligence. It is like the sunlight of Eternal Truth bursting through the clouds of obscurity and bathing all life in a celestial glory. It is the Absolute with which we are dealing and nothing else."

– Ernest Holmes, *The Science of Mind*

Intelligence Is My Way

In this joyous celebration of life, I know there is only One Mind, One Power, and One Presence. This power is infinite in its expression. It is moving and circulating as me. My mind is Divine Mind. It knows what to do and how to do it.

I allow the light of this truth to bring clarity to every situation in my life. I act with wisdom in the choices I make regarding health, relationships, and financial matters. I let go of any guilt, fear, worry, and indecision. I allow the Truth to set me free and recognize that my life is unfolding perfectly. I release all judgments and act from love.

Recognizing that the universe is abundant, bathing all of life in Its celestial glory, I open myself to freely receive Its gifts, knowing with absolute certainty that it is all good and all God. Intelligence is my way, and today is my day of acceptance.

For this awareness, I give thanks and release this word to the Law of Mind. And so it is.

"I came from greatness. I must be like what I came from. I will never abandon my belief in my greatness and the greatness of others."

– Wayne Dyer, *Change Your Thoughts-Change Your Life*

Greatness Is My Way

In the Allness of God, eternity dwells. The One Infinite Mind, the Source and wholeness of being, opens me to this new awareness. I am one with the One, and since I came from greatness, greatness is my way. As I accept this Truth of the indwelling Presence.

I accept my success and live with ease and joy. Today is the day I express my divinity through my work, my relationships, and my health. I will never abandon this belief.

I celebrate myself and the greatness in others. I release any thoughts that block this Divine flow, and I know that all is good, and all is God. All of my needs are met and my good unfolds perfectly.

I give thanks for this revelation and release this word to the Law of Mind. And so it is.

Carol Lynch

"This Science is not for the timid, it is for the daring…
it takes spiritual courage to change your mind and keep
it changed."

– Raymond Charles Barker,
The Science of Successful Living

I Proceed in Wisdom

In this sacred moment of now, I recognize the Truth. There is only One Mind, One God, and One Creative Intelligence. It is the unfolding action of intelligence as me.

In this awareness of the oneness of being. I am lifted up to where I belong. By knowing and recognizing the Power and Presence of God within me, I celebrate the courage to change my mind and proceed with the wisdom to keep it changed. I recognize that a Power greater than I inspires and ignites the light within. Allowing my gifts to touch all and letting go of yesterday's beliefs, I choose only what works. Richer thinking expresses as my richer living and moves the greater adventure of life to my everyday experience.

I rejoice in the abundance life offers. Praising all the experiences that have brought me to this realization, I know I am an expression of God in action. For this insight, I give thanks and celebrate. I let go of the small and assume the great. And so it is.

"You can resume your life when you create the bearable from the unbearable."

– Dr. Tom Costa

Chapter 3

Creating the Bearable

For years, as a working mother, I juggled my job, raising my child, and pursuing an alternate career. I began in the public school system as teacher. Later, I became a school psychologist, and eventually, an administrator in a new school district. It was only after I completed all the licensing requirements for psychologist and when my son was finishing high school that I committed to pursuing the ministry.

As a woman in a male-dominated society, it took more time, dedication, and training to move ahead in the schools, and I found similar challenges in ministry. That being said, motherhood is the most rewarding and the most challenging of all life choices.

My son Eric, a gifted computer programmer and web designer, presented me with many joys and many challenges, as any parent understands. His passing on December 5, 2016, was the saddest and most unbearable day in my life.

I was visiting my cousin Liz in Waretown, New Jersey. She woke me at 4:00 a.m. to tell me that Carl, Eric's father, was on the phone, and it was an emergency. When I asked Carl what happened, he said, "Eric is dead."

Stunned, I replied, "No, it can't be. How can Eric be dead?"

I told Carl I would be home later. I could not possibly drive at that moment. I was in shock. My only child.

When I left for Waretown the day before, Eric was fine. He was recovering from a routine surgical procedure and appeared to be well. In fact, a friend was with him when I left, and they were planning to go to the mall to buy computer parts for a laptop Eric was repairing. My son hugged me and said, "See you tomorrow, Mom."

I was numb. Liz suggested, "Call your Pastor; it may help." So I phoned Rev. Wade and shared the news. It was early in the morning when I called, and I woke him up. He expressed surprise, asking me, "What happened?" He said he would help with the memorial service and suggested I call him back when I arrived home.

I drank several cups of tea as I shared my disbelief with Liz. She reminded me that Rob, her only child, had been gone for ten years. Then she stated, "I still grieve."

My disbelief, in part, stemmed from the fact that Eric had been doing so well in recent months and had survived two previous accidents. A year earlier, he had totaled two cars within a span of a few months, escaping with minor injuries and short hospital stays.

All the time I kept thinking, This can't be happening. Times of such significant loss are defining moments, particularly when the loss is so unexpected.

Ernest Holmes wrote:

> I believe in the continuation of the personal life beyond the grave, in the continuity of the individual stream of consciousness with a full recognition of itself and the ability to know and to make itself known.

From eternity to eternity, Eric is gone, but he remains forever in my heart. His spirit is with me. He also left a son––my grandson, Eli––who is now eight years old and is so much like his father.

I miss Eric. He brought joy and adventure to my life. I still feel his presence here. Dealing with his unbearable, unexpected death is not easy.

My cousin Liz helped with the arrangements for Eric's funeral. He loved being in Clifton, New Jersey, with my parents and his cousin Adam. I made funeral arrangements for him there.

Rev. Wade conducted the service, and the ministers from First Church participated. It felt like bringing Eric home.

I still cry tears in silence. At the time of this writing, it is February, two years later. I have found comfort with the Spiritualists, who have taught me to look for signs of Eric's presence and have restored my belief in eternal life. I discuss this in more detail in Chapter 10.

Gordon Smith, world renowned medium and author, stated:

> Our spirit is forever. The spirit world will persist in bringing this message to us, through mediums and other means, until we learn that death is nothing to fear because it does not mean the end. Death is but a change; it is the doorway into forever. This I know beyond reasonable doubt.

Grief is love, and not something that leaves quickly. It is a process that unfolds and becomes a part of you. Any parent who had lost a child knows this. Restoring our faith and seeking comfort is a process.

One door closes and another door opens. Life goes on. We choose our new direction. Having a spiritual belief helps. Knowing this brings inner peace.

Spiritual Mind Treatments for Creating the Bearable

"Sail on silver girl. Sail on by, your time has come to shine. All your dreams are on their way. See how they shine . . ."

– Paul Simon, "Bridge Over Troubled Water"

It's Your Time

There is a Power in the Universe that is for good. It is the One Mind expressing as Oneness––One, One, One.

It is the awakening to the Divine Presence deepening within me. The Christ Consciousness that radiates peace, love, and joy. The light shining as faith keeper. It is time.

All that is necessary for Divine Right action in today's affairs expresses now. I open to this spiritual knowing and rejoice in the discovery.

Letting go of fear and releasing what no longer works, I celebrate the harmony and unfolding action of love guiding me right now. Today is the day to be the dreams, to let them shine. To move forward, onward, and upward into the abundant life.

Feeling the warmth and kindness, I know that it's all good and all God. This is the truth, and it is the way. This word is released to the law of mind. And so it is.

"We now let go of everything and enter into a state of peace."

— Ernest Holmes, *The Science of Mind*

Peace Is My Intention

In the infinitude of Life, there is only God, only Good, and only love. It expresses as me in peace. Recognizing my oneness, I awaken to knowing the Truth of my being.

As God in action in this moment, I let go of everything and enter into a state of peace that blesses all I meet today. I declare this as my new attitude. I move into the loving flow of Spirit, knowing all my needs are met. There is joy in my home, my work, and wherever I go. I am always kind, and I expect the best from others and myself.

The power of love propels me forward into a joyous expansion of consciousness. I free myself from any past experience that disturbs my peace. I am confident Truth is expressing as me. Love lights the way, and I accept the peace that allows me to move into the silence of my soul.

I am truly blessed by the power of love, which provides me a joyous life filled with delight. It is all good, and it is all God. For this, I give thanks. And so it is.

"Let us forget the past and live in the eternal present of God's happy smile."

– Ernest Holmes, *The Science of Mind*

I Live in the Now

God's presence is all there is. It is the Infinite stretched in smiling repose, the One Creative Intelligence unfolding and expanding in this moment. It is God in expression as me.

Celebrating this day of love, I feel Spirit's embrace. I affirm my oneness, my joy of life, and my discovery of the freedom to choose. I know Divine Right Action takes place and opens the door to forward movement in life, bringing peaceful resolution to any challenge I face. Recognizing this power within and the majesty of my being, I gratefully release and forget the past.

Divine circulation refreshes my thought with new actions for prosperous, joyous living. As I freely give, I freely receive. I know only good lies ahead, for it is present now and always.

I give thanks for this awareness and reside in the eternal present of God's perfect essence. I let this Truth set me free. And so it is.

"Love is the miracle cure. Loving myself works miracles in my life."

– Louise L. Hay

Chapter 4

The Power of Love

Hearing Dr. Raymond Charles Barker on the radio inspired me to become a practicing Religious Scientist. *Treat Yourself to Life* is one of Dr. Barker's most popular books. In it, he discusses the importance of love.

Loving ourselves is the way to self-esteem and success. Making our subconscious mind our best friend is the first step in the process. In our prayer work, love is the key factor.

What is love? Ernest Holmes defines love as, "the self-givingness of the Spirit through the desire of Life to express Itself in terms of its creation."

Dr. Barker tells us that love is not enough; it's the one thing we can never get enough of, and the one thing we never give enough of. Love is the necessary expression of living life to the fullest.

I am not talking about love as a religious term or the kind of love that has to do with sex. True love is the barometer of our happiness, and we experience it in proportion to our ability to give ourselves to others.

Lonely is defined as a sad state, one of unnecessary isolation. Lonely is lonely wherever we are. Unhappy is unhappy. Loneliness is a serious thing. If someone is experiencing loneliness, it was probably a pattern in childhood. Something new now triggered it out of that person's subconscious mind.

During childhood, we can feel lonely even in large families. Our busy parents may not have understood our needs if they were preoccupied with adult issues.

Most people do not realize that loneliness has a spiritual dimension. Being in our physical form can seem lonely and claustrophobic compared to the vastness in which our spirits originated. This feeling is completely natural, although it isn't acknowledged in parenting classes and traditional psychology.

The realization that the material world cannot take away our loneliness can make a difference. How? By our recognition that we are not alone.

Science of Mind teaches that acknowledging that a higher power is always with us relieves tension and allows us to see that we are never spiritually alone. We are always connected to something greater.

The spiritual antidotes to loneliness are meditation, spiritual mind treatment, listening to our intuitive self, focusing on gratitude, practicing mindfulness, and helping others. Our spiritual journey is always an individual one, yet it doesn't have to be lonely.

Love in the spiritual sense is not sentimentality; it is the cohesive action of the universe. It is what holds things together. Love is the power that draws ideas together and holds them in right relationship.

There is a law of attraction. It is a law of cohesion in the universe that not only keeps things together, it also draws people together——people who are of like mind, people who share values and enjoy being in each other's company.

The law of love has the power to draw together those with similar interests, like playing tennis, collecting antiques, dining out, swimming, attending movies, owning a pet, or discussing books. This is why I suggest to my clients who are seeking a loving relationship to list all the qualities they would like in a romantic partner and to become those qualities themselves. Then, they will attract what they are seeking.

In mind, ideas group together under a cohesive law much as things do in the material world. Lonely people tend to live in the past; as such, they have nothing to give to their present world. One way to change this behavior is to focus on something new and different and consciously begin to live in the present.

If you are lonely, do a spiritual mind treatment declaring that love is in circulation in your life. Affirm that this love is flowing to you, through you, and from you to others in your life.

Learning to love is the key to effective spiritual mind treatment. We cannot treat in a loveless state of mind. If our mood is negative, we will not see results. Our state of consciousness determines the effectiveness of our treatments. The atmosphere of successful treatments is love. Love is the quality that makes us feel we are at one with all.

We love people who respond to life as we do. Love is the feeling that we are at one with someone and with life. Love is a beautiful feeling, precious like a summer breeze or the scent of jasmine or the smell of freshly cut grass.

Even so, in this oneness, we must leave the other person free to be as he or she desires. "Lovers must be like the pillars of the temple and stand apart," wrote Kahlil Gibran.

When we love, we must love enough to allow the other person to make mistakes. We must learn to love ourselves despite our mistakes. We've all made them, and probably will make more.

This is where Science of Mind teaches us to have the courage to face the situation and find solutions. There is an order in the universe; there is law, and there is love. When you love, you let everyone use the law of mind in his or her own way.

The key is to make love the center of your life. Yes, we must be more loving–– but we also must be wiser, more orderly, and more law abiding. The law of cause and effect operates whether we like it or not, whether we believe in it or not. It will respond to us as we respond to it. It receives, reacts, and creates. Love without this type of order is confusion.

At the basis of God consciousness, we are all one. If we accept this as truth, it follows that every person is part of us, and each of us is part of everyone else. How does it feel to consider that every person in your present world is some part of yourself?

Every individual who is living now, has ever lived, or ever will live must exist somewhere at this very instant. One of the "places" they exist is within us. Another place is Eternity, or, as described in the Spiritualist teaching, Summerland.

When we love someone, we are loving a phase of our own being. When we disagree with someone, we are disagreeing with a part of ourselves. We are all one in God, and we are all expressing a unity in diversity.

As we give the people in our world the freedom to be themselves, we must also claim our own right to be ourselves. Trying to reform others does not work. We can't change other people. When we let go of a person and relax, right action takes place. Divine intelligence operates more freely for us if we are not trying to superimpose our ego on other people.

God's divine uniqueness is spiritual variety functioning at different levels of consciousness. We may have similar points of view, we may sit at the same desk, speak from the same podium, or attend the same church, yet we still have our differences. Why? Each of us has a divine essence that is ours alone.

If we believe we are all born out of love, that inner something that makes everything live, we can learn to get along with others by seeing the Divine Presence within. We cannot change others; besides, it's not up to us. We must allow infinite Spirit to operate through each person in his or her own individual way.

What others want is none of our business. It's not up to us to be anyone's savior. We can't force personal relationships; we must let them develop.

Are you aware that you have never really selected a friend in your life? Friendship happens. If people are not drawn to you by right of consciousness, they will never be your friends. If we want to know what our own state of consciousness is, we can tell by looking at our friends.

Quoting Kahlil Gibran once more, "let there be spaces in your togetherness . . ." Let there be room between you and those you love so that each may express his or her own unique gifts.

Spirit's nature is to create variety, to keep life an exciting adventure. If we are going to get along with people, we must take them as they are and not try to change them. We can only change ourselves. If we are willing to work within ourselves until we have changed our concept of others, they will appear in our world in a different way, and our reaction to them will be changed.

Let us experience our good right now and live in that place of freedom. Each one of us is in our right place, and now is the right time to create our good. It's time to take back our power and release any inner bondage of fear or superstition.

Our personal economy is based on love. The more love we give, the more love we have.

Spiritual Mind Treatments for Love

"Let us seek wholeness above all else."

– Ernest Holmes, *The Science of Mind*

I Am Filled with Joy

In this moment of now, I know the truth. There is One Mind, One Power, One Presence, and One Love. This loving action of Spirit is all there is, and it is the indwelling presence within me.

I am filled with joy at the thought of oneness. I know my life unfolds as love–– the love that carries me forward in this day to the truth of my being. All my needs are met as I let go and allow. I release any unpleasant encounter that generates negativity or judgment. I let divine guidance lead me to my rightful place. I deserve only the best, and I accept my good right now.

Today, I seek wholeness in all matters––health, relationships, finances, creativity, and action. I move forward in right thinking and love. Remembering that whatever I give comes back to me multiplied, I give with love and receive with joy.

I give thanks for this greater awareness. I release my word to Law. And so it is.

"Mind, then, reveals to us, not something to get but something to give, something to reveal, something to radiate."

— Tom Johnson, *A Fountain of Truth*

I Give Love

In the allness of God, where eternity dwells, the One Infinite Mind radiates love. It is the loving action of God unfolding as me. It knows what to do and how to do it. Lovingly, it celebrates life as me.

I let my feeling of completeness reveal all the joy, beauty, and creativity life is. As I freely give of myself and let go of any need to "get" anything, I allow my good to happen. I release any self-rebellion of past choices and move into my new beginning right now.

Recognizing the Divine Presence within me, I flow in harmony with those in my world and move into unity with all life. I realize every day is a new beginning. This is the day I let my love shine and resonate with the magnificence of God that I am.

I am thankful for my enlightened thinking, which expresses as radiant love. This is the letter or Truth; I know it, and I live it. And so it is.

"Prosperity is the ability to do what you want to do when you want to do it."

– Raymond Charles Barker, *The Power of Decision*

Chapter 5

Developing a Prosperity Consciousness

Prosperity is. It's all around us, everywhere we go.

We live in an abundant universe. We are as rich as we ever shall be right now. Why?

We are spiritual beings, and the power for good is within each one of us. The door to more money or health or creative ideas is always open. We have to feel worthy and think that we already have. It's the law of attraction, and it's always working in our lives. We have to be thankful for what we have, because whatever we bless, praise, and focus our attention on expands in our lives.

Prosperity is a verb. We live prosperity when we make it a habit that works for us.

How do we start?

First examine your core beliefs about money. Is your thinking negative or positive? Take the time to congratulate yourself every time you catch or correct any negative thoughts or thinking patterns, such as, "I can't afford that," or, "Money doesn't grow on trees."

The way to increase prosperity is to take charge of your mind. Express your gratitude daily for all that you have. Life's purpose is to be exciting and know the Good will always last, as the Good is infinite. Expect the good, every day! Before you leave your home, affirm: I expect only good today.

If we see life as a struggle, we have to change that belief. We have to believe something else. Otherwise, the law of attraction will only bring us more struggles. Welcome your challenges, they help you grow. Express your gratitude for what you have.

It's very important to remove lack consciousness. It usually stems from childhood beliefs. Negative beliefs are like poison. Check if you have any of these in your thinking patterns: complaining, blaming, gossiping, regrets, self- criticism, or envy.

These thoughts take away your power and diminish your feelings of self- worth. If you are responsible for it, you can change it. If you blame others or deny these thoughts, they will stick with you like Velcro.

Change your thinking, change your life.

We learn the art of changing our mind to eliminate thoughts about failure. We shift our thinking to possibility: "I can." It's a time to remove our habitual thinking on loss, lack, and limitation, focusing on richer thinking and success.

When we succeed, we can help others. We are never too old. Louise Hay started her publishing business at age 60. At age 82, she co-authored a book with Dr. Mona Lisa Schultz entitled, *All is Well.*

We have the power to control our thoughts, and they determine what is attracted to us. We have to develop the desire to be something better.

Napoleon Hill said this: "Money consciousness means that the mind has become so thoroughly saturated with the DESIRE for money, that one can see oneself already in possession of it."

We all have Divine Natural Authority. All the power is in each one of us. We have to use it to experience its effect.

Money is not the power, it is a means for experiencing more of what we desire in life. Dr. Barker affirmed that we must love money and appreciate it. Being powerful makes us the money.

Prosperity is everywhere, money is available, and we have to be equal to it. It all depends on your prosperity consciousness. What do you believe?

Money comes from everywhere. Do you consider yourself worthy? Maintain a constant atmosphere of worthiness. Know that today is your turn. Make God personal. Affirm often: "This is good for me, and I can have it."

There is nothing between in God and me. We are one and always connected. We have to love money and have fun with it. As children, many of us experienced the joy of a treasure hunt.

At Eastertime, when I was a child, my parents would hide eggs with money in them. When I became a mother, I hid eggs with money in them for my son to find. I now do this for my grandson.

As adults, it is important to have fun with money. Many people enjoy digging for treasure or panning for gold. I have collected antiques for many years, and I derive great pleasure from using my money this way.

What is your favorite way to have fun with money?

If the answer is, "I don't have one," or, "I don't know," start thinking about ways to change this. Doing so will shift your thinking in positive and constructive ways.

We have to pay attention to our thinking and to what we may uncover in our minds. We have the ability to change our thinking and reframe or eliminate any negative thoughts.

What do you think of yourself? Do you feel you are worthy? Know that you deserve good.

We have to be responsible and do the work, as money does not drop down from the sky. Sitting around and thinking you are rich may be a start, but you have to have the feeling as well.

We start where we are and begin to express gratitude for what we have and who we are. Knowing we are enough, we develop the consciousness—the mental awareness—to put our desire into action. The law of attraction always works, and a negative thought can never attract a positive result. We have to be fearless, stay aware of our feelings, and expect only abundance.

Whether we complain or are grateful, we are right. The universe always says yes. The law of mind receives, reacts, and creates.

We must know that we are responsible for our good by way of our consciousness. Consciousness is mental awareness of our thoughts, our feelings, and our emotions.

The silent power of attraction is irresistible. Get yourself out of the way. The next time you look in the mirror, look into your own eyes—do you see beauty and love? Affirm: "My life always unfolds for my highest good. I believe I am worth it." There is abundance in everything.

Rev. Wade Adkisson stated, "The quality of your thinking always reflects the quality of your life." How would you describe the quality of your thinking? Do you think of yourself as valuable? Do you think of yourself as worthy of all good things?

Find the good in everything by looking for the good in everything. Imagine for a moment that there is a celestial piggybank––and you have unlimited access to it!

We are the believers, we are not the belief. It is done unto us as we believe. The good news is, beliefs can be changed. Shift your thinking to the positive and change your experience. Know that your beliefs create your experience. Use your mind for good. Think good: "I am happy now!"

What is belief, and is belief enough? The dictionary defines belief as: "A state or habit of mind, a conviction that certain things are true. An opinion, expectation, or judgment. A creed or doctrine, religious faith, trust or confidence."

Ask yourself: What is the truth surrounding my personal beliefs? Do I believe I am too old to try something new? Do I believe I can change?

Many people worry that there isn't enough good to go around. Worry represents a belief. And our beliefs are impressing on an intelligent activity all the time. Dr. Barker wrote, "Trouble results when an unintelligent factor is introduced into a field of intelligent activity." In this case, the "unintelligent factor" is our belief in anything other than the abundance of good.

There is a power for good––do you believe this? Are you consciously aware of this truth at all times? Sustaining this level of awareness requires mindfulness. It must become a practice.

We have to decide what we want to impress on Divine Intelligence on a daily basis. We must shift the focus of our thoughts to what is true––to what works––and stay in spiritual balance.

As a starting point, try this exercise: Take one of your beliefs and prove that it is true and prove that it is false. See all sides of every position. Notice what emotions arise.

Try not to judge yourself too harshly. Remember, the beliefs themselves are impersonal. We are the believer––not the belief.

Our self-talk is powerful, and how we use our minds is important. It is easy to argue against something, yet there is power in being able to see both sides. Do you really believe what you think you believe?

God is greater than anything we can put in our way. We have to weed out the subconscious stuff that works against us. The mindset we hold colors the world around us. This science works.

Our beliefs are changeable, and we have the freedom to choose. When our beliefs are in alignment with the truth of God, we know it. Life is always evolving into good and more good. The power is in our use of mind.

Practice believing that your finances are always secure. Eliminate thoughts of lack and limitation through the use of affirmations and spiritual mind treatment.

God is the source of all supply, and it is unlimited. It is non-negotiable. Separate any old negative beliefs from what you now want to believe. You have the power of mind to do this. There is a place within each of us that knows what to do; this is the truth of every person, including you.

Do not give your power away to other people in your life—past or present. Release any belief that doesn't serve you.

Sometimes our beliefs are bullies. Recognize those bully beliefs and affirm the truth for yourself.

How would your behavior change if you really believed that God is source? Choose affirmations that work for you, that you believe and know. Don't try to change things; release what you don't want with love. Remember, what we resist persists.

When we move ourselves into a state of peace and gratitude, solutions appear. Allowing ourselves to love naturally and feel gratitude for the good we experience brings an expansion of good into our lives.

We have to pay more attention to what we believe than to what we are doing if it's not working for us. When we know what we can do, and when we know who we are, we can do what we need for the right result. We are one with God, and each one is the magnificence of Spirit in expression.

How much do you really want, and what are you resisting? If we send mixed messages to the Law of Mind—in essence introducing an unintelligent factor into the Universe's field of intelligent activity—we will not demonstrate our good. We must decide how much good we want, and how much we are willing to receive, and focus on those positive intelligent thought patterns.

How do you think about money, and what is your relationship to it?

If, for example, we worry or are afraid that money is running out, or that we don't have enough, we are sending a mixed message. If we fear the thing we want, it cannot and will not manifest.

We must provide the consciousness of what we want. Our belief sets the stage. Prosperity consciousness requires us to embrace it all.

The misuse of our mind is a habit and it comes from a belief that our good is conditional. We must free ourselves from the habits that cause lack. Mixed messages create mixed results. If we catch ourselves complaining, we are sending out a mixed message.

Prosperity simply is. It's always present. We get what we are willing to take. Try living your life from the inside, knowing your good is unfolding perfectly, no matter what. This is the spiritual truth.

Rich is the beauty of life, and we have to be comfortable with wealth. The next time you go shopping, buy yourself something that makes you feel rich. Take note of the feeling. Affirm, "Rich is my inner truth."

Continue to examine your beliefs on a regular basis. Are you thinking richer thoughts or reverting to those old thoughts of lack?

Take a new action in your life and throw away the negative limiting ideas. Be consciously aware of your thoughts and step it up a notch.

There's more to do and more to be. Set your goals, do your forgiveness work, make the commitment to your practice, and watch your prosperity consciousness grow.

Expect your good. Choose prosperity now.

Spiritual Mind Treatments for Prosperity

"The world is advanced only by those who more than fill their present places."

– Wallace D. Wattles

I Think Rich

There is One Creative Intelligence in the Universe. It is the Infinite Mind of God, the All-good. It is eternal in expression and limitless in time and space. I live, move, and have my being in the One Mind.

Relaxing in this Truth, I accept the Divine Flow of substance that enriches and prospers me today. As I observe my thoughts, words, and actions, I contemplate only the beautiful, the infinite potential of my unlimited Source.

I release any thoughts that may limit me or cause me to think about past mistakes, recognizing no mistakes have been made. Accepting all I am, I embrace whatever I do each day with diligence and love. Blessing the good I have and giving thanks for my ability to exceed present expectations, I more than fill my present place. I give more, I think rich, I think success, and I think love.

I expect the best as the world is advanced by my awareness of a greater, grander demonstration of life. This is the Truth of me, and I rejoice in the joy it brings. And so it is.

"The Infinite is a divine extravagance. It is forever giving Itself away.

– Raymond Charles Barker, The Power of Decision

I Am Prosperity and Peace

In the action of this day, in the peace of this moment, I recognize only God and only good. I seek what is right and true and celebrate my oneness with the Infinite. I am spiritual efficiency expanding in consciousness as prosperity and peace.

Today, I accept my good, knowing the Universe is unlimited in supply. I decide to live a richer life. I allow Spirit to guide me to the ways and means to have it all now.

Any past concept of limitation, lack, or loss is released once and for all. The Truth sets me free to know abundance is my birthright. I am a perfect idea in the mind of God. As I release any shadow of negative thinking, I know I am worthy of all good. As I look for the beauty and feel the love in everyone and everything, my mind opens to the creative process as I see the Infinite as a divine extravagance.

I freely receive God's gifts and give thanks for the joy expressing as my richer life. This is the Truth for me. And so it is.

"No matter how much good you experience today, you should expect more tomorrow."

– Ernest Holmes, *Can We Talk to God*

I Expect More Good

In the Infinity of Life, eternity dwells. It is the One Infinite Mind, One Power, One Presence. It's all Good, and It's all God. It is the unfolding action of Spirit. And all this is It expressing as my life. It unfolds perfectly right now. Moment by moment, and allows me to experience greater wealth, greater love, and greater peace. It allows me to see Good in every situation.

Seeking expansion, I quickly and easily release negative thoughts. I know the divine Presence within guides me at all times and in all experiences. I let go of anything that contradicts my growth and awareness. I move forward in the light of Love, knowing all of my needs are met.

I expect more good, no matter how conditions appear. I choose what is right and true for me. I embrace the Divine within, recognizing that it is holding me. I listen for the inner voice, knowing that as I find God, I find myself.

For this new acceptance of Truth, I give thanks and allow peace and harmony to be my way. Today is filled with good, and tomorrow brings even more. I declare it so. And so it is.

"There is a power for Good in the universe and you can use it."

– Ernest Holmes

I Have the Right to Be Prosperous

There is One Mind, One Power, and One Presence. It is all Good and all God, expressing as me. It is the One Infinite Mind as my mind today. It is perfect Intelligence guiding me for good.

In this sacred moment of now, I know the Truth, and I allow the divine flow of riches to move to me as I open myself to freely receive the gifts of God. Everything I do prospers as I accept my right to be prosperous. I let go of what no longer works. I express thanks for the riches I already have. I release all fear and doubt.

My new awareness of the Divine Presence within me moves me in this day to know the truth of me as a mighty moving power of God in action. I express this with a new spiritual confidence that propels me forward. I accept and know that I deserve only the best, as my life is the unfolding action of Good. Abundance is everywhere. I prosper in everything I think, say, and do.

I give thanks for this day and for my new awareness of Truth. I release this word to the Law of Mind, knowing that as I partner with the universe, my experience is success leading to greater success. And so it is.

"Our individualistic culture inflames ego and numbs
spirit."

– David Brooks, *The Second Mountain*

Chapter 6

Jumping into Spirit

D r. Ernest Holmes maintained it is far easier to teach the truth than to practice it. Practicing it means we must jump into Spirit. We have to wake up to the truth of our being.

We were programmed to find the perfect career, perfect mate, and perfect living space. We set out to be that success. We found life to be a training ground that offers us choice.

Life takes discipline. Most of us have the tendency to resist change, and only when we use said resistance as a signal or impetus for change do we face the dissatisfaction and wake up!

This is divine discontent telling us to slow down and pay attention to the nudge. It is the Divine urge.

In general, our personal growth and evolution is motivated by inspiration or desperation. If we have a predisposition toward self-inquiry, we will find our defining moments popping up in a delightful way. They will lead us to actions that honor Life. They will be answers that put us on a course of action that affirms the presence of a prevailing power for good that lies within us.

A tool for discovery of our higher self is silence. Silence is a compass that can guide us to our center. It is a sacred medium through which we may fathom the infinite depths of the original self, a sacred continuum eternally offering itself to us.

We don't have to embark upon a quest to find silence. It is a matter of uncovering it right where we are. Meditation is the simple tool anyone can use to move into the silence.

Tools are required to make life changes. Such tools include daily spiritual practice, spiritual mind treatment or prayer, meditation, time to reflect, and making an investment in ourselves.

We must look at life in a new way. As we do, we see the bigger picture, we feel connected, and we sense our oneness. We avoid knee-jerk reactions to people, situations, and circumstances. We break the cycle of negative thoughts and fill our minds with new images.

Life is no longer a series of random joys and mishaps; rather, it becomes an interactive experience constantly offering us the choice to understand and master ourselves. We cannot change others; we can only change ourselves and our reactions to others.

We have to face our shadows and mistakes and look at the experiences that have caused pain, sadness, and guilt. We recognize that every person, regardless of appearances, is a responsible adult who thrives in the world—as are we. Seeing ourselves and others this way frees us to respond from Truth instead of reacting from judgment.

We reward ourselves for this self-examination through self-care and self-love. Perhaps we write a goodbye to the past, keeping cherished memories and letting go of anything that causes shame or guilt. We may nurture ourselves by doing things that make us feel good, such as taking a relaxing bath, having a massage, reading a novel, or drinking a cup of tea.

To nourish our soul, we might talk things over with our friends or see a therapist or Spiritual Practitioner. Anything that assists us in unlocking life's passion and meaning is a positive move in the right direction.

When our memories are negative, they hold us back. Erasing the troubling story and focusing on something new will free us.

Thought plus feeling equals consciousness, and the conscious mind has the power to change subconscious mind. This has been proven in experiments with biofeedback and in imagery used in sports psychology. Things are not always as they appear.

During our journey, we discover the magic of our soul. We are all one, yet each is a unique individualization. Our goal is to become more aware of what we are and to expand our consciousness.

When we bring a sense of renewal into our lives by recognizing that we are spiritual beings, we begin to live life as a great adventure, and we have the courage to be. We allow a new enthusiasm into our daily lives and express ourselves as the magnificent radiance of the Divine.

We can change anything in our lives for the better because Conscious Mind has the power to change the fixed beliefs we hold in subconscious mind. Why not free ourselves to a greater, grander expression of life?

Spiritual Mind Treatments for Change

"Spiritual Mind Treatment changes consciousness
and initiates a new mental causation that overlays the old
effect . . . lifting our thinking out of the ordinary into the
extraordinary."

— Wade Adkisson, *Sacred Sundays*

I Am Super

There is a Power in the Universe that is greater than I am. In my recognition of this Truth, I understand God is all there is. I realize I am at one with the One.

I now use this Power to lift my thinking out of the ordinary into the extraordinary. I am of God; therefore, all I am is God in expression. Beauty, joy, and love circulate in my thoughts as I move through this day expecting only the best. Anything that appears to limit my greater demonstration of life is released. I find Truth within, and whatever I need to know is revealed.

Realizing something grander is ever available, I devote my thinking to the extraordinary and let it radiate as me. Today, I experience something more joyous and wonderful than anything I have known before.

Through my blessings, I know my way is God's way, and I celebrate my perfect demonstration of life. I am super. For this I give thanks. And so it is.

"Fame if you win it, comes and goes in a minute...
Love is the answer."

– Jimmy Durante

I Celebrate Success

I recognize a Power and Presence in the Universe that is Infinite in Its expression. It is all God. It is all good. I am one with It. Success is the way, and I accept this as the truth of me.

Truth sets me free to create new avenues of prosperity, love, peace, and joy. New ideas circulate through me, bringing to me a deeper awareness of the Divine Presence within. I celebrate my success. I let go of any past failure or loss and recognize that my potential is unlimited.

Love is the answer. Love is the power and love lights the way for a deeper spiritual realization and the awareness that with God, all things are possible. I no longer depend on myself alone, knowing Divine Presence within always supports me. My new attitude about life reflects as success and luxuriates in the love that I freely give and graciously receive.

I am a loving expression of the One Life and I accept the joy it brings to me and all in my world. I live the good life. Successful living is my way today, and I celebrate it now. I am grateful for my change for the better. And so it is

> "Through your faculty to imagine the end result, you
> have control over any circumstance or condition."
>
> – Joseph Murphy, *Believe in Yourself*

I Imagine the Best

There is a Power and Presence in the Universe, and It is for Good. It is ever expanding in my world as my experience of love. This love unfolds as people, places, and things, enhancing my life each moment.

I live from joy to greater joy. I experience love and greater love. It brings to me the wisdom of my way today. All it is, I am. As I declare this to be the Truth of me, my world expands to the greater, grander possibilities of life. Any thoughts of loneliness or sadness are released with my new awareness of Truth.

As my imagination dares to dream the dream, the Power within me allows me to embrace love and be the joyous receiver of God's gift. And so it is.

"Spiritual healing can occur in any aspect of your life. Healing can be of the mind, body, emotions, or circumstances. Surrounding you (relationships, work, finances, life goals)."

– Dr. Stuart Grayson, *Spiritual Healing*

Chapter 7

The Path to Healing and Forgiveness

E rnest Holmes tells us that spiritual healing is based on the concept that there is an inner presence of complete perfection at the center of everything. There is a Creative Mind Principle in nature that reacts to our thoughts and feelings, causing some form of manifestation in our lives.

We believe that when this Creative Spirit dominates our actions, and when we are in conscious and harmonious unity with It, we shall automatically clear the psychological passageways. We were meant to be whole, happy, and well.

We seek to clear any obstructions from our subconscious mind that inhibit or block the creative flow of life. We must consciously be one with Source. In our oneness with Source, we must recognize our oneness with others.

For example, when consulting a medical professional for help with a condition, seeing everyone involved as one with Source and one with us benefits our healing process greatly. In this way, doctors, nurses, psychologists, and dentists, to name a few, are agents of God as they carry out the necessary procedures to allow our healing to take place.

We have to accept that we live from God. There are three things we can come to understand:

1. We have a whole, perfect, and complete spiritual body that in itself is never ill, diseased, or disturbed.
2. We are endowed with a conscious mind that can interpret this spiritual body, either correctly or incorrectly.
3. This interpretation determines the condition and experience of the physical body.

In *The Science of Mind*, Ernest Holmes wrote, "The fact is, no matter what we believe, there is a Divine Essence within us that never changes." The basis of spiritual healing is a recognition that we have a spiritual body that is perfect and immutable. It is the gift of life. We each possess a subconscious storehouse of memory that is the sum total of all our thinking.

We put all kinds of information into our subconscious storehouse. The good news is that we can take information out, too, through the use of Science of Mind's form of prayer--spiritual mind treatment.

Subconscious mind, or soul, is the entirety of all of our thinking. It largely decides what is going to happen to us. It is the automatic medium between God's perfect pattern and our experience of it.

Spiritual healing is not a contest of wills or the power of suggestion. We are not psychics or mediums. It is a method of mentally unifying with something that already exists, that something being a perfect state of spiritual wholeness.

In spiritual healing, we have to adjust our perceptions so that the picture is clear, and, hence, the truth is brought into focus. In his book, *Spiritual Healing*, Stuart Grayson tells us, "Spiritual healing brings about change in our world of experience by changing consciousness."

We adjust conscious mind to see through the blur of subconscious reactions and the fog of our memory to the Truth that is. It works with the Law of Life.

Behind all of this, there is a clear picture of what it "looks like" to be one with the One, a wholeness that can be seen, felt, and understood. As we consciously begin to think about the wholeness of our being, we manifest the health, radiance, and vitality of the living Spirit within. We properly begin to adjust the lens of the mind to clarify the spiritual body. We move the mind into alignment with the Divine Reality that exists at the center of our being.

We, of course, must be convinced that this is so. All is as we believe. Affirmative thinking will uproot and deny any negative thoughts or ideas. We do not hesitate to contradict and refute any unreality or anything that appears less than perfect, such as illness or lack.

We must know with complete certainty that treatment, our word, is the Law of Good, and actually does remove that which it denies. It brings into manifestation that which it affirms.

A psychologist or psychiatrist would never probe the depths of memory to relieve the scars of an emotional block unless he or she believed that behind that block was a whole and complete person. The spiritual practitioner also proceeds from the belief that each person is already whole, perfect, and complete.

The practitioner does not assume that he or she is the healer; rather, the healing is the revealing action of Spirit. The practitioner works to remove certain mental and emotional blocks and make certain mental adjustments that permit the spiritual body to energize the physical. We speak the word, and God receives, reacts, and creates.

Our faith has made us whole. When we stand in an attitude of complete acceptance, without fear or doubt, we can watch the blessing happen.

We begin with the fundamental promise that there is a universal intelligence, which is the creative principle in the universe, and that this intelligence exists everywhere. God is all there is. All great religious systems have sensed this and believed in it: One Universal Intelligence that flows through everything and without which nothing could exist.

All manifestations of life represent gradations of the One Intelligence. The Creative Principle acts as a mirror, reflecting back to us the image we hold in front of it. It was the high mission of Jesus to show us how to use it. He was the great way-shower.

Carol Lynch

Jesus used the Creative Principle. He asked those who came to him for spiritual healing, Do you believe I can do this? When they answered in the affirmative, he affirmed, "Be it done unto you as you believe."

One of the first techniques in spiritual healing is to clear the mind of our own thinking. The practitioner has the faith and confidence in his or her own word. He or she must believe that the Law of Good operates in, on, and through what has been thought or said.

We have to cultivate the faith of God and know there is no difference between prayer and its answer. Then we will believe that we already have received what was prayed for, and the demonstration is made.

Spiritual Mind Treatments for Health

> "It is not easy to turn from a disease and know that there is disease, when we know very well it is an expression of the moment."

> – Ernest Holmes, *The Science of Mind*

Perfect Health Is Mine

Today, I rejoice in my good, recognizing the One Power and Presence in my life. It is Creative Intelligence unfolding as me and expressing as perfect wholeness. As I assimilate this truth, I believe there is but One Life, and that Life is expressing as me. It is whole, perfect, and complete— Perfect God, Perfect Being.

I know this is so. This thought refreshes and energizes me. It reminds me I am a mighty moving power of God in action. In this new awareness, I deepen my spiritual knowing and reveal the Divine Presence. I release any congestion or confusion, recognizing there is no truth to the appearance of this momentary condition. The spiritual idea of perfect health moves through every facet of my being. The Divine's circulation of Love through all of my body allows me to know my perfect health is right here and right now. I celebrate the elimination of any negative thought or idea.

Letting go of any disease, disorder, or discomfort brings a change for the better that results in revealing the health that is already mine. For this, I give thanks and celebrate this moment of realization. This is the Truth, I declare it so, and I release it to Law. And so it is.

"You forgive by releasing the energy of fear and resentment that arises when you perceive that you have been wronged in some way . . . you are healing yourself by releasing the negative energy that whatever occurred has occurred and you are ready to move forward."

– Jim Lockard, *Sacred Thinking*

I Heal and Forgive

Today, I celebrate life and let the power and presence of the Divine move me into a deeper awareness of Truth. Recognizing that love is the power––the power at the heart of Infinite Mind––I allow that love to unfold as me. The indwelling Christ consciousness reveals the absolute peace, love, and joy within, and I express it in my daily life.

This presence manifests in all my activities and in all I meet. This love is infinite and eternal. Releasing any fear or resentment that arises from negative thoughts, I move forward into new creative activities that enhance my being. The spiritual idea of wholeness moves through me now and brings about change for the better.

New experiences, new vistas, and new ideas create a feeling of joy, peace, and excitement. I allow something greater and grander than anything I have experienced before to happen now. This is the Truth, the way, and the perfect right action, here and now. And so it is.

Carol Lynch

"Illness is the body's way of telling us that there is a false idea in our consciousness. Something that we're believing, saying, doing, or thinking is not for our highest good."

– Louise L. Hay, *Experiencing Your Good Now*

Healthy Living Is Mine

There is but One Life, and that Life is my life. That Life is whole, perfect, and complete, and It supports me in every way. I am at one with Life, and I make choices that reflect healthy thinking and healthy living.

Every part of my being is an action of joy, a surge of enthusiasm that upgrades my consciousness. As I assimilate this truth, I feel a new zest for living, and a new excitement about who and what I am. I am a perfect pattern in the mind of God.

I release any false ideas in consciousness that would out-picture as illness or disease and eliminate any beliefs that block my healthy thinking. As I change my belief, I change my life. New thoughts bring new actions that express as a healthy me. I affirm my good and select only those ideas that promote greater health, greater wealth, and greater love.

I experience my good now! For this, I give thanks and rejoice in my healthy mind and body. This is the Truth. I celebrate it, and I accept it. And so it is.

"I realize that I live in the midst of a Creative Intelligence that receives the impress of my thought and creates my life experience from that thought."

– Wade Adkisson, *Sacred Sundays*

Perfect Health Is Revealed

There is One Power, One Presence, One Mind, and One Law—God. It is the I Am individualized and expressed in me. In subconscious mind, the pattern of perfect body is at its peak.

This treatment is the word of God. It is uncovering and revealing the perfect pattern of body. Being the word of God, it now destroys all other body patterns and any false beliefs that may have been added or attached to this perfect pattern. This Divine pattern of body is now reactivated by the spirit and is now manifested in outer expression. It is the only pattern of body that operates in me and expresses its perfection.

Rejoicing in this perfect body, I give thanks for it. I know this impresses my thought to create a healthy life experience. This is the Truth, known and declared here and now. And so it is.

"What you are thinking about now is creating your life . . ."

– Rhonda Byrne, *The Secret*

Chapter 8

The Law of Attraction

I was out recently at Aldo's restaurant in Wyckoff, New Jersey, which was one of my sons' favorites. I ran into an acquaintance, Suzanne, whom I had met during a previous visit to the restaurant. That time, she had noticed my sad state. We talked about my son's death, and she gave me her dragonfly earrings.

It is always a pleasure to see her, and this time, she gave me another gift of a bracelet. She mentioned that she was very excited about a book she was reading entitled, *The Secret*. I told her I had taught the premise of the book at my church in New York, and that the law of attraction is part of the Science of Mind teaching.

It struck me that this was a synchronistic event. As such, I decided to include the law of attraction as a chapter in this book.

My late pastor, Rev. Wade Adkisson, taught this idea every Sunday: "The quality of your thinking determines the quality of your life." That which we contemplate we become.

If we are unhappy, we can change that through spiritual mind treatment. We know the law works through consciousness, not just through words.

In his book, *Spiritual Healing,* Rev. Adkisson's predecessor, Dr. Stuart Grayson, tells us that spiritual healing is a change in the consciousness of the individual. All change, all transformation, begins within; it must be the result of a change of consciousness.

Our lives reflect our consciousness. Our health reflects our consciousness. How well do we care for and respect ourselves? Our ability to love reflects our consciousness. Our treatments, or prayers, must reflect feeling. The great mystic, Judge Thomas Troward, declared, "The feeling is the law, and the law is the feeling."

Illness, for example, is a temporary state of consciousness. It reflects our thoughts and beliefs.

How do we know what the state of our consciousness is?

Look at your friends, not your family. We look at our friends because we made a conscious choice to bring them into our lives. We may have selected our parents before we were born, but it was not on a conscious level. Relationships are mirrors of our self-esteem. They afford us the opportunity to look at ourselves.

In *The Science of Mind,* Ernest Holmes explains that we don't claim disease is the result of thinking. One negative thought doesn't result in disease; however, prolonged negative thinking does, as thoughts have power.

Every word has some power within us. Divine potential is ever present, ever available. The word we speak is the law unto our lives.

How do we put *The Secret* into practice in our lives? First, we have to deepen our relationship with Spirit by choosing to treat or pray before making decisions instead of after the fact.

Our second responsibility is to choose actions that promote our greater good and the greater good of others. Are we reacting out of fear, or are we promoting harmony in the situation?

Each one of us is a divine being, and we are individualizations of God in action. We are always using the law of attraction, as we are what we think about. What we think about and focus our attention on expands and manifests in our lives.

The universe always says yes to our requests. That is why it is so important to recognize what we are thinking about and what we believe. When we practice principle, we can turn our lives around and experience the good we desire. We are not in the business of changing others; we are working on ourselves.

In *The Secret,* we are told to "Ask, believe, and receive." This does not always work because there may be ideas in our consciousness that need to be dealt with or released before a new experience can take place.

We have to **know** the truth for us, not just idly believe. We must use the concept of allowing to take place and be in the flow, be the thing we desire.

If we are seeking more love in our lives, we have to be more loving. First, we have to love ourselves more. When we have self-love, we can give our love to others. We never run out of love; the more we circulate love, more love returns to us.

If we desire more money, we must develop the consciousness to receive more and the wisdom to keep it in our lives. Money has to be circulated. There is a law of reciprocity that governs this: As we give, we receive. It is important to understand our attitudes and beliefs about money and examine them. Many of them come from our childhood and the beliefs of our parents.

We are where we are in life through our own actions, whether we are conscious of them or not. We are fully responsible for ourselves and our situation.

The good news is that we are not bound by any mistakes of the past. Those were lessons to be learned.

We always have the capacity to change. We have the freedom to think, and we can learn to think about ourselves in a new way. We can change our lives by changing the way we think.

We have to discover the treasure within ourselves to become aware of our connection to the Divine Presence within. We have to jump into Spirit, the "aha" moment when we realize that the thing we have been looking for is within. It is not something out there. It is the secret place that lies within each one of us.

In the words of Emmet Fox, "The secret place of the most high is your own consciousness, and this is the most important practical discovery in the whole science of religion." By recognizing this divinity in all, we come to a new appreciation of ourselves and the world. In this way, we begin to experience God and build our spiritual awareness.

To do this, it is necessary to have faith and to trust the process of life. We can begin with a small change. When we do this, the results are the demonstration and the proof we seek to believe.

Each one of us can put *The Secret* into action in our lives. We can take the first step right now in this moment. As an ancient Egyptian inscription reads: Moments turn into minutes, minutes into hours, hours into days, days into months, months into years, and years into lifetimes.

Why wait? The choice is yours.

Spiritual Mind Treatments
for Creative Living

"This day, like every day, is a new beginning. It is filled with a wonderful potential of new ideas and new inspiration."

– Willis Kinnear, *30 Day Mental Diet*

Today Is the Day

The One Infinite Mind—One Spirit, One Power, One Life—is all there is. It is my life now. It provides me with purpose and an outlet for love to express. Creative Intelligence as my activity allows me to open myself to a greater, grander way of life.

Today is a new day. I am filled with the joy of living and the celebration of self as new ideas that promote my new prosperity. As I release the past, I no longer entertain any nonsensical thinking. I move into living my life on purpose, feeling inspired and appreciated.

As I freely give more to my world, it joyously gives back to me. In this reciprocal action, I let go and let God inspire me to healthier, happier, and richer living—a life filled with love, friendship, and correct thinking.

For this new beginning, I give thanks. I celebrate my good right here and right now, as today is the day. And so it is.

"The true freedom of spiritual fitness comes from letting go of our preordained behavior and creating a vibrant new reality afresh each day.

– Caroline Reynolds, *Spiritual Fitness*

I Have the Power

In the awareness of this moment, in the beauty of this day, I recognize the One Power, the One Presence, and the One Life in expression as me. I rejoice in the realization of my unity with all there is.

I exercise the power spiritual fitness brings me. It energizes me to live in Truth and trust, which results in a vibrant new reality each day. I let go of any preordained habits that might hinder my growth and forward movement. I practice my new behavior with joy and expansion.

I move forward into a deeper recognition of the Truth of my being, releasing what no longer works and opening to a new understanding of myself. I accept a higher mastery of who and what I am—a mighty, moving power of God in action. I relax in knowing I am on a journey filled with love, which moves me into a greater realization of the beauty of my life.

I take this opportunity to share the joy and express my gratitude for the magnificence of Spirit, which I am. This is the Truth I release to Law, knowing I have the Power. And so it is.

"Being one with the Creator of all things, I joyously individualize the ever-flowing, never-ending Life of unlimited creativity."

– Nancy Fagen, *It's a Divine Done Deal*

Chapter 9

Everything Begins with an Idea

L ife works from the inside out. This reminds me of so many of the mystery programs on television, such as *Midsomer Murders,* when one detective says to his partner, "This looks like an inside job." Well, of course it is, as all life is an inside job. Everything begins with an idea.

Our ideas have great power in our lives. They are the initiating factor in everything we do. They are the building blocks of our lives. I had to have an idea to write this book, and, obviously, that idea took form (otherwise, you would not be reading this).

At times it is rather startling when we realize how easily we allow outside influences to manipulate and impinge on our thinking and, by extension, our lives. For example, I might turn on the television or radio or ask Alexa for the weather report and hear that there is a chance of rain later today. As such, I may decide it's going to be too much trouble to drive to New York City to meet a friend at our favorite restaurant, so I forget it, since I do not like driving in rain.

We must realize that our thinking is always operating on multiple levels of our conscious and subconscious mind. There are four levels: physical, emotional, intellectual, and spiritual/ethical.

The first and most dominant level is the physical. How we feel in our body. If any physical ailment is bothering us, it will always take precedence in our thinking. If we have a headache, stomachache, or toothache, for example, the feeling of physical pain or discomfort will take priority over what we are formulating as ideas.

The second level of consciousness is emotional. Are we feeling happy, joyous, energized, and open and receptive to our greater good demonstrating in our lives? Or are we depressed, feeling low, or lacking the energy or ambition to move at all? We see that our emotions play a very important role in our thinking.

Thirdly, we are always operating on an intellectual level, deciding what is best for us to do. However, this level will always take a backseat to our physical and emotional levels of consciousness.

The fourth level is our spiritual and ethical level. What is right for us to do? What is for our greater good? If—and I mean *if*—we can empower our consciousness on the spiritual level, we can override all the other levels. We can change our beliefs, perceptions, and acceptance of life, all for the better, through the empowerment of consciousness.

Since we are always operating on all four levels, we must understand that any idea literally had to pass through each of these levels to reach the light of day in our conscious minds:

1. Through our physical level, through our feeling of wellbeing.
2. Through our emotional level, through our balanced emotions.
3. Through our intellectual level, through our acceptance that this idea is worthwhile.
4. Through our spiritual level, through knowing the idea supports our spiritual beliefs and does not violate any of our ethical standards.

Only when it meets all of these standards, can we declare, "I have an idea!" The study of the Science of Mind teaching is an empowering one.

Empowering in that we take control of our thinking as we discipline our patterns of thinking toward the greater expression of living in joy, peace, love, and abundance.

As we empower ourselves, we experience a feeling of dominion. We don't take dominion over other people; we take dominion in our ability to choose, to evolve, and to move forward and grow in absolute freedom.

We take dominion over our own thinking, thereby controlling our own actions and evolving in our own consciousness. When we do this, sacred connections are made as the right people move into our world. The right situations move into our experience, and the people who do not belong in our world leave.

What was once right for us may not remain the same. We release the old to make way for the new, knowing the Law of Growth is always expressing in our lives. We must see that there is a Law of Creativity operating in our lives––operating as the Law of Attraction––attracting new people, new opportunities, and new experiences.

The study of Science of Mind is a process of coming to understand that we always have been Divinely Connected. We have forgotten this truth. We may have unknowingly disassociated ourselves with this great power. Hence, we must be patient in our studies, for spiritual truths are often rather abstract ideas, and it takes time and patience to learn them.

Many of us search for happiness and abundance, yet our search never seems to rise above the physical level. If we do the same thing in the same way, we get the same result over and over again.

Learning to identify ourselves with the good we desire––and working from the inside, recognizing the Divine Presence––reveals a proven psychological fact as well as a metaphysical truth: That with which we identify ourselves tends to be drawn into our experience.

The Law of Attraction tells us that we live in a reflective universe. As such, what we "reflect out" returns to us.

This Law is always operating, whether we deliberately use it or not. To use it deliberately and effectively, we need discipline.

We must discipline our thinking and our study. We must set aside time each day for our spiritual wellbeing. Over time, we learn to work effectively and remove ourselves from the world of the ordinary and move into a world of enhanced living. We move from where we are to where we have never been before, knowing that if there is no investment there can be no return.

We must expect to demonstrate the best out of life because we usually get out of life just what we expect to get. We want the best, the better, and the greater demonstration of good to take form in our lives. What do you believe you deserve?

The phenomenon of consciousness is very important. The deeper we investigate and inquire, the more we realize consciousness is not only very important, it is the only thing that is important.

It may be difficult for some of us to accept the idea that our perception determines our reality of life. It is often challenging to accept and understand that our beliefs, our perception, and our consciousness literally create our life and our enjoyment of the life we create.

Our attitudes create our experience. Our perception of possibilities determines our opportunities. It follows that how much love, how much joy, and how much success we have is determined by our own perception and by our own consciousness.

Throughout history, successful individuals have been able to think big and to perceive greater ideas. The things that are possible only become possible because someone perceived the possibility.

The Creative Principle of the Universe––with or without our approval, and with or without our conscious knowledge––is receiving the impress of our thought and acting upon it. This means as far as the universe is concerned, our secret inner life is not so secret, for we are always demonstrating our consciousness in outer life.

At all times, we are demonstrating our prosperity consciousness, our consciousness of good, and our consciousness of love and joy! Our lives tell on us because our lives reflect the content of our consciousness.

We must realize that the Divine Presence is forever desiring our greater good. It is forever supporting us in our forward movement in life. We must embody this as the Truth of our Being. There is God and nothing else, the Divine Presence that is Infinite and Eternal.

Only we can empower our own consciousness. No one else can do this for us. I share this Truth with you, but only you can accept it and embody it.

Why? Life is an inside job, and only you can do it for you.

Spiritual Mind Treatments for Creativity

"I am pure Intelligence always acting intelligently."

– Raymond Charles Barker, *The Power of Decision*

I Trust and Respect Myself

The One Infinite Mind is all there is. It is the unfolding action of the great Divine Intelligence, the Creative Power in the Universe. I am one with It, expressing as pure intelligence in all I think, say, and do.

Divine circulation moves through my every thought, producing expansion into the Infinite as the joy of creative thinking blesses me. I release any obstacles to this new action. As I awaken to the Truth of oneness, I am set free to soar in greatness and expression of the magnificence of my being. I trust and respect myself, knowing as I honor myself, I honor all. I see the Divine Presence within and celebrate my discovery of this Truth.

I express gratitude for my life. In this act of awareness, I feel the Presence of Spirit within and let my love flow. Poised in peace, I choose intelligent thinking as my way. And so it is.

"No matter what you are doing, you know the originating power is in your action. You stand on Principle."

— Robert Bitzer, *Collected Essays*

I Stand on Principle

In the silence of this moment, in the beauty of this day, I sense the Power and Presence of Spirit. Recognizing there is only One Mind, I know my mind is one with the Mind of God.

Spirit expresses as me in my every action. I take time to reflect on my oneness and the Truth that God is all there is. I enjoy every conversation with loved ones and friends as I go about my daily work. I express love and the commitment I make to myself and others in my world. I befriend myself and know right thinking is my way to right action.

I take the time to celebrate myself and stand on Principle in all I think, say, and do. Today is the day of discovery of my rightful place. My purpose is clear, and I accept that every ending is a new beginning.

I take action right now to be all I can be, knowing I am an individualization of God in expression. For this, I give thanks to the Divine Presence within. And so it is.

"God exists in everything. God exists in me, and because God exists in me, I am able to recognize other beings in whom God exists."

– Ernest Holmes, *The Science of Mind*

Chapter 10

What Is Your Concept of God?

In Science of Mind, we teach that it's all God and it's all Good. God is energy, a force, a power within; it is not a bearded man in the sky watching everything we do.

What counts is what we do with our power. Whatever you are doing, lean in to the concept of being Divine. Do not depend on other people or your resume.

What are you willing to be? Be busy being the embodiment of God, the Good. It's what is in our hearts that counts—the inspired vision of ourselves, the essence of all that is.

Mellow in the truth of seeking your highest and greatest good. If you are not where you desire to be, love more. Think and know that life is *for* you. If you want to forget about something that happened to you, forgiving is what helps. Forgive yourself, and forgive the transgressor. Embrace the idea. Do not allow a grudge or resentment to rent a space in your mind. Don't be immersed in regret over past mistakes. Get bigger ideas about God. Give it greater meaning in your life. Go for more than simply finding a parking space.

Benjamin Franklin once said, "However difficult or humbling our mistakes might be, it is ultimately wrongness, not rightness, that can teach us who we are."

Know the God within you. It is energy, the inner voice, the light, and the Divine urge.

Believe in yourself. This principle works. It has worked for me and for many of my clients.

Demand more and know. If you feel stuck, do a spiritual mind treatment for something that is not emotionally charged, something that's just fun for you—and expect it to demonstrate!

The law of attraction described in Chapter 7 works. God does not know what is going to happen to us until we make up our minds. There is but One Life, and I *am* because I make choices that become the circumstances, conditions, and events in my life.

If I don't like what's happening, I have the power to change my idea. And so do you.

We treat to have the consciousness of the thing we desire, to embody it. For example, we do not treat for money; we treat for the consciousness of it, the circulation of it in our affairs.

Let the world see the teaching expressed in your life. We have to *be* what we desire; not just talk about it, but also walk the walk. It is a way of life, as we live in a universe of our own thought.

Be reborn in the now. What we give out is what we receive in return. Be a blessing to yourself, and make every moment count. Be all you can be and express it for others to see in your daily acts of generosity, kindness, and appreciation for all life.

Ask yourself, What have I decided about life? Am I content to sit on the sidelines, or am I moving into action on my desires?

When we do our treatment/prayer work, we treat for ourselves first, then we treat for others. As we give, we receive, and we can only give to others what we have. Celebrate yourself and be the Divine Presence in action.

Spiritual Mind Treatment is an affirmative form of prayer. It is the great gift from the great metaphysical teacher, Ernest Holmes. Simply taking your thought and feeling and directing it so that your inner self—the inner law, which is God itself at the center of your being—may move through you and bring something fresh and new. This is called the creative process, and whether you believe in it or not, it is happening.

We have to watch our thoughts, keep our consciousness centered on good, and recognize the spirit of mind that is within each one of us. Each of us is really a law unto ourselves, and this works in our favor when we free ourselves from the opinions of others, when we free ourselves from world opinions or the fears of the collective consciousness.

As we establish new patterns, they work their way out in our lives. They are our experiences, our health, our wealth, our relationships, our work, and our way of living.

Spiritual Mind Treatment transforms and renews our minds with fresh ideas. It is what we think and feel each day, moment by moment, awake and asleep. When we consciously choose the way we use the law of mind, we realize there is nothing prayer cannot accomplish. Spiritual Mind Treatment is a powerful tool. Use it wisely, and rejoice in the demonstrations.

Spiritual Mind Treatments for Clarity

"For where your treasure is, there will be your heart also."

– Matthew 6:21

I Am Awakened

I know and recognize that there is One Life. That Life is God, that Life is good, and that Life is my life, now. I awaken to the Truth of my being, that the Divine Presence is within. It is the treasure. It is the joy.

I see the glory and the grandeur of God's gifts operating through me and celebrating my oneness. I express gratitude for these gifts and open my heart to allow the light within to shine and radiate my inner peace.

I am an outlet for the prospering action of God as I release the beliefs that have limited me. I open to a new faith in the infinite supply of Good that is everywhere. I freely receive the gifts, as I know I am worthy of the best. I rejoice in my discovery of the Truth that sets me free. It is a wonderful thing to be me.

I give thanks for this day. I am grateful for the spiritual awareness of my connection to the One that empowers me to openly accept and receive this Good. Knowing that there is but One Life, I allow the treasure of my heart to be me in expression. I let the way of my heart be the heart of my way. I release my word to law. And so it is

"I am…what I am because of my consciousness . . .
finding God in every moment."

– Holmes and Barker, *Richer Living*

I Find God

Knowing there is only One Life, and that life is God, I celebrate the Truth of myself finding God in every moment. Today, I embrace the new, the greater, and the grander possibility of Life. In this joyous recognition of Truth, I find and celebrate myself.

My mood is one of love and an unfolding action of peace that frees me to change my thinking and my life for the better. As I liberate myself from the past, from my old habits, I allow love to be my way. I transform my thinking to reflect only good and only God. Each moment offers this opportunity for a new thought. Any false ideas are replaced with creative thoughts, which expand my world, reminding me that with God, all things are possible. There is nothing to limit me.

This is my day. This is the resonating of Spirit in all I think, say, and do. I have faith that my desires are God's desires, and I am all I imagine. And so it is.

"Quiet your mind, open your heart. Let your inner Light shine."

– Robin Bennett, *The Journey Within*

Chapter 11

The Journey Continues

When we reach enlightenment, or what author David Brooks calls our "second mountain"––a life of love, care, and commitment rather than one dedicated to seeking material gain––we seek the spiritual meaning of life. We have made a commitment to ourselves and to the God within. As we embrace our losses, we know that life goes on.

To regain my strength and confidence, I explored the idea of eternal life. I came across a book called *Bridging Two Realms,* by John Holland, which led me to The Journey Within Spiritualist Church in Pompton Lakes, New Jersey.

I attended a lecture given by Rev. Janet Nohavec on a Saturday morning in May, 2018. The topic was "How to Communicate with Your Lost Loved Ones." Those present were paired with other attendees and asked to close our eyes and think of who was tapping us on the shoulder. My partner said that a young male who liked books, loved the ocean, and was surrounded by seagulls was there in Spirit. She said he mentioned to her a garden in the back of my home. My partner and I did not know each other; we had just met at this workshop. My son had planted a special garden in the backyard of our home two years before his passing.

Rev. Nohavec then instructed us to keep a journal and choose our signs for the presence of our loved ones. For Eric, I selected a deer, a cardinal, and a rabbit. For Wade, a butterfly and a blue jay.

It's a comfort to have the reminders along with the fond memories. As a Religious Science minister, I am aware of Ernest Holmes' strong belief in the afterlife. The Spiritualists dig deeper with the work of mediums and have a history going back to England, which further enhances the belief in immortality and the continuity of the soul.

One of the classes I taught at First Church with Rev. Joyce Jackson was entitled, "Who's Afraid of Thomas Troward: The Creative Process in the Individual." In the class, we discussed Troward's view on eternal life, as well as the view of Ernest Holmes.

Troward gives us many descriptions of death. His secret to eternal life is based on the subconscious mind and the impressions we make on it. He suggests we must impress upon the subconscious the thought that in passing over to the other side, we bring our conscious mentality with us. Ernest Holmes, on the other hand, tells us that life is ongoing and we retain our consciousness and move into a greater expression of livingness.

In Judge Thomas Troward's last will and testament, he specified that upon death, he be cut in four places by a certified practicing surgeon in the presence of two adult witnesses. His reason was to be assured that he would not be buried alive. It was reported by his daughter, Ruth Troward, that after having spent a morning gazing at the painting he loved, he had passed to the Great Beyond without illness or pain.

Rev. Adkisson made his transition on April 13, 2018. On September 29, 2018, I attended a seminar at The Journey Within Church entitled, "Where Two Worlds Meet, an Evening of Mediumship with Brian Robertson and Simon James."

Brian Robertson asked the audience of about one hundred people whether anyone could relate to the spirit of a gentleman from Georgia, who had horses in his youth, who had a connection to Pavarotti, and who had traveled to Venice? I raised my hand because that description fit Wade.

Wade had a horse during his childhood in Georgia. He was well acquainted with Luciano Pavarotti, as his partner, William Hudson, worked as a manager for the Metropolitan Opera. Wade also traveled to Venice during his world tour. Brian Robertson said that Wade's spirit was letting me know he was active on the other side and was sending his message of love.

I know many are skeptical of mediums, yet I experienced a message from Wade from the spirit world. Brian Robertson did not know me, and none of the information about Wade was on social media. It was an awesome experience, and I conclude that Ernest Holmes is right about the afterlife.

The thought that our lost loved ones will greet us in Eternity is comforting and affirms my faith in the Science of Mind teaching. I am also reminded of Holmes telling us to be open at the top.

Spiritual Mind Treatments for Expanding Consciousness

"There is a place in us which lies open to the Infinite; but when the Spirit brings Its gift, by pouring Itself through us, It can give to us only what we take."

– Ernest Holmes, *The Science of Mind*

I Am Open to the Infinite

There is one Universal Intelligence, Life Force, and Source back of all creation, and that is Spirit. Recognizing there is a power for Good in the Universe, I know this power is Infinite in Its expression and is the unfolding action of Perfect Intelligence. This Intelligence operates through me, moment by moment. It sustains and maintains me in the perfect expression of life within Its Divine embrace.

Universal Intelligence makes itself available in my ability to think clearly and to make right decisions. I give expression to that which is Infinite and boundary-less to create in my life. I release any thoughts of limitation. I accept my greatness. I know the Truth of me is only Good. I expect the best, and I graciously receive the best. Out of the Divine givingness, the greater abundance of Good flows to me.

There is more love, more health, more financial freedom, and more joy in my living. It is the Divine in action as me, and I rejoice in knowing that this is the Truth—life is not limited. I open myself for the taking and joyously receive Spirit's gifts. This is the way it is. I am ever grateful. I release my word to the Law. And so it is.

"Your greatest asset is the ever-present action of God in your Life."

– Norman S. Lunde, *You Unlimited*

I Am Unlimited

In the infinitude of Life, I know there is only One Mind, One Power, and One Presence that transcends all. It is God in action as me. It is the One Mind common to all. It expands as I think thoughts of Good, of God.

I realize this ever-present action propels me forward into the greater, grander demonstration of Good. I do not allow world beliefs in loss, lack, or limitation to operate in my life. I dismiss them right now.

Recognizing my acceptance of this Truth propels me forward in this moment to openly receive my gift and to express it as my way. Today is my day. Today is God's Day, and I rejoice in this asset as Life supports my choices, allowing divine right action to take place.

I celebrate my Divine Heritage and use it with wisdom. I give thanks for the love, peace and prosperity expressing as the givingness of Spirit flowing through me right now. And so it is.

Appendix

Honoring Louise Hay:
A tribute given by Rev. Dr. Carol Lynch at
the Sunday, September 3, 2017
Meeting of The First Church of Religious Science New York

As many of you are aware, Louise Hay made her transition on August 30, 2017, dying in her sleep of natural causes.

I began that day with my spiritual work, breakfast, then attending to my emails and the church website and Facebook page. August 30, 2017, was the second anniversary of the transition of Dr. Wayne Dyer. Facebook had posted my memory photograph of Wayne Dyer, Louise Hay, and Shelley Anderson on my page. I commented about my memory of Miraval Spa in Tucson, Arizona, where I attended Dr. Dyer's seminar on, "Ten Secrets to Inner Peace and Success." It was there that I first met Louise Hay in January of 2002.

Later that afternoon (August 30, 2017), I received a message from Elena Urban that Louise Hay had made her transition. I was stunned; it was exactly two years from the date Wayne Dyer had passed. They were friends for more than 30 years, and-she joined him-synchronicity. Wayne Dyer always said, "There are no accidents."

Louise told me about her time at First Church and invited me to lunch with her personal assistant, Shelley Anderson. Louise sent me clients over the years and referred many to First Church. Rev. Adkisson remembers her visit to our church on 48th Street. She would stop into our bookstore, check out which of her books we carried, then inspect the ladies' restroom and complain that Dr. Grayson hadn't painted it.

Louise had a difficult early life filled with violence and abuse. She dropped out of high school at age 15 and ran away from home in Los Angeles. She eventually made her way to New York City and became a successful fashion model. In 1954, she married Andrew Hay, an English businessman who introduced her to a world of status and wealth. He left her after 14 years.

Feeling despondent, Louise walked into The First Church of Religious Science at 14 East 48th Street in New York City and found a new direction for life. She was a student of our founder, Dr. Raymond Charles Barker, and took classes with Lynette Tucker and Bernice Carter. Rev. Jane Brendel and Rev. Eric Pace were also there at the time. Louise was close to Lynette who went for lunch and beauty treatments with her between classes.

Louise was struck by the expression, "If you change your thinking, you can change your life." She attended the church twice weekly and felt like a whole new world opened up for her. She became a Religious Science practitioner and workshop leader. From this work, she published her first book, *Heal Your Body,* which later became her international bestseller, *You Can Heal Your Life.*

She went on to form Hay House, her own publishing company. In a feature article in the May 4, 2008, edition of the *New York Times Magazine,* she was named Queen of New Age and was noted to be one of the bestselling female authors, alongside JK Rowling and Danielle Steel. However, she topped them by being the only one with her own publishing house.

Louise was named Spiritual Hero of the Year in 2009 by *Science of Mind Magazine.* Her key message was to love yourself. She believed that loving the self was the key to life. Her work with AIDS brought her into the limelight, as she held the Hayride workshops when many others were fearful of working with those with HIV and AIDS. She was interviewed by

Oprah Winfrey regarding her work and Hayrides. She taught the Science of Mind principles in her "I Can Do It" workshops and Hay House World Summit, as well as her many books, CDs, and movies. She spread our teaching far and wide.

Louise believed that our thinking creates our life, and she developed many books of affirmations to help us keep our thought positive. About prosperity she said, "I deserve the best and I accept the best now." In her book, *Inner Wisdom—Meditations for the Heart and Soul,* she affirmed, "I am on an endless journey through eternity."

> *In the infinity of life, all is perfect, whole, and complete. There is a time of beginning, a time of growth, a time of being, a time of withering, or wearing out, and a time of leaving. This is all part of the perfection of life. I sense it as normal and natural, and though saddened at times, I accept the cycle and the rhythms. Sometimes there is an abrupt ending in mid-cycle. I am jarred and feel threatened. Someone dies too soon, or something was smashed and broken. However, I know that life is ever-changing. There is no beginning and no end, only a constant cycling and recycling of substance and experience. Life is never stuck or static or stale, for each moment is ever new and fresh. Every ending is a new point of beginning.*

– Louise Hay

A Tribute to The Rev. Dr. Wade Adkisson

Rev. Adkisson enriched the lives of so many. The news of his unexpected death deeply saddened me. I first met him when he became pastor of the prestigious First Church of Religious Science New York, following the retirement of Dr. Stuart Grayson. I had been introduced to Religious Science by Dr. Raymond Charles Barker through a radio broadcast entitled, "Yesterday Ended Last Night."

I took some classes with Dr. Stuart Grayson and occasionally attended Sunday meetings at Alice Tully Hall. Wade awakened me to the beauty of our teaching, and I enrolled in his classes. Rev. Jane Brendel encouraged me to become a practitioner and to participate on the Board of Trustees. It was a great adventure. At the time, I was working in the Waldwick Public Schools as Director of Special Services and heading the district's Crisis Response Team.

Wade began his career in the business world. He held many degrees, including a doctoral degree in Egyptology from the University of Chicago's famed Oriental Institute. He traveled to Egypt numerous times and took members of First Church on two tours. He loved to travel and went to Europe frequently. He and his partner, Bill Hudson, who was manager of the Metropolitan Opera, dined at Paul Bocuse's restaurant in Lyon with Pavarotti. Paris was one of Wade's favorite cities. He loved New York, and we celebrated many occasions at Tavern on the Green. He was a connoisseur of fine dining and wines, and we enjoyed many of New York's finest.

I assisted him with his book, *Sacred Sundays,* and at his request, I developed and maintained the church website with my son, Eric Lynch. Wade was devoted to the teaching. He received his training from Dr. Stuart Grayson. He tells the story of how he was amazed at Dr. Grayson's success with a woman's hand, which was instantaneously healed. When he asked him how he did this, Dr. Grayson replied, "Wade, you jest. We treat for the "spiritual idea."

I was part of Wade's last ministerial Class, which was co-taught by Rev. Joyce Jackson, Senior Minister. Six of us became ministers: myself, Rev. Judith Byrd Bullock, Rev. Theodora Parker, Rev. Michael Sternlieb, Rev. Robert Villanova, and Rev. Veronica Wright. Wade accompanied us to the Fort Lauderdale Church for our ordination hearings in March of 2014, which were followed by a ceremony at Lincoln Center where he was assisted by Rev. Jackson. He was proud of us, and we appreciated his mentorship. He taught with clarity and integrity.

Wade's Sunday meetings at Lincoln Center were on Principle, always. Practitioners provided treatment prior to his talks. Soprano Viviane Marie Mordo lifted hearts with music, often accompanied by Cameron Carpenter, Katya Sonina, or Alexander Itzbitser. It was a joyous celebration of life.

Wade's favorite quote was, "The quality of your thinking reflects the quality of your life." He left a legacy of love and a dedication to the principles of the teaching of the Science of Mind. A bright light left us for a new journey. As Ernest Holmes wrote, "They are not dead, they have but found new songs to sing. New life and laughter there to bring to love's eternal spring."

Wade lives on in the hearts and minds of all those whose lives he touched. For me, he changed my life for the better and will always be a part of me.

Rev. Dr. Carol Lynch

Suggested Reading

Alive and Ageless by Maxine Kaye (Maxine Kaye, 2012)

Beyond Reasonable Doubt by Gordon Smith (Coronet, 2018)

Bridging Two Realms by John Holland (Hay House, 2018)

Good Grief by Theresa Caputo (Simon & Shuster, 2017)

It's A Divine Done Deal by Nancy Fagen (Nancy Fagen, 2014)

Life! by Dr. Tom Costa (Dr. Tom Costa, 1988)

Magician to Mystic by Brian Robertson and Simon James (Tellwell Talent, 2017)

Power Thoughts by Louise L. Hay (Hay House, 2005)

Sacred Sundays by Wade Adkisson (Xlibris, 2006)

Sacred Thinking by Jim Lockard (One Spirit Press, 2010)

Shortcut to a Miracle by Michael C. Rann and Elizabeth Rann Arrott (DeVorrs & Company, 2018)

Spiritual Healing by Dr. Stuart Grayson (Simon & Shuster, 1997)

Stake Your Claim by Emmett Fox (Harper & Row, 1952)

10% Happier by Dan Harris (Harper Collins, 2014)

Ten Secrets for Success and Inner Peace by Wayne Dyer (Hay House, 2001)

The Art of Abundance by Dennis Merritt Jones (Tarcher, Penguin Random House, 2018)

The Creative Process in the Individual by Thomas Troward (DeVorrs & Company, 1991)

The Miracle Club by Mitch Horowitz, (Inner Traditions, 2016)

The Power of Decision by Raymond Charles Barker (DeVorrs & Company, 1996)

The Science of Mind by Ernest Holmes (Science of Mind Publishing, 1938)

The Second Mountain by David Brooks (Random House, 2019)

Treat Yourself to Life by Raymond Charles Barker (Dodd Mead & Company, 1954)

Where Two Worlds Meet by Janet Novhavec with Suzanne Giesmann (Aventine Press, 2010)

Your(Re)Defining Moments by Dennis Merritt Jones (Tarcher/Penguin, 2014)

Printed in the United States
By Bookmasters